BLUNDERS,
GAFFES and
OWN GOALS

First published by Carlton Books in 2014

Carlton Books
20 Mortimer Street
London W1T 3JW

Copyright © Carlton Books 2014

A CIP catalogue for this book is available from the British Library.

ISBN 978-178097-586-3

10 9 8 7 6 5 4 3 2

Printed and bound by CPI Group (UK) Ltd, Croydon, CR0 4YY

Other hilarious football titles from Carlton Books include:
The Big Book of Football's Funniest Quotes
Being the Gaffer! The Crazy World of the Football Manager
1001 Bizarre Football Stories

BLUNDERS, GAFFES and OWN GOALS

THE FUNNIEST AND DAFTEST SPORTS QUOTES EVER!

Edited by Adrian Brady

CARLTON
BOOKS

Contents

Introduction

On the face of it, the role of the commentator and pundit must seem like the easiest job in the world. But watching sport and talking about it, as you will find out in the pages of this book, is a verbal minefield.

Let me begin by saying that commentators, broadcasters and pundits do a fantastic service in relaying the key incidents and finer details of the great sporting events to the masses, however, it doesn't always go as planned and this book is a celebration of their occasional vocal mistakes and hilarious gaffes.

Whether it is a confused cliché, mixed metaphor, unintentional innuendo, babbled banter or a statement of the unbelievably obvious, these brilliant quotes bring an added dimension and sense of humour to the sports we love...

Athletics

Perhaps the purest of all sports as competitors bid to go "higher, faster, stronger" than ever before. The sport's commentary calamities have a beautiful innocence about them too, with broadcasting legends David Coleman and Ron Pickering setting the standard for comic gaffes.

Athletics

" False start from Darsha – it was almost
as though she went before the gun went. "
**Athletics commentator Paul Dickinson
seems unsure of the principle of false starts**

" She's letting her legs do the running. "
**A detached view from athlete turned
commentator Brendan Foster**

It's a lovely sunny day here in the studio.
Channel 4 athletics presenter Ortis Deley

" He's 31 this year. Last year he was 30. "
BBC commentator David Coleman

" The Italians are hoping for an Italian victory. "
David Coleman

" The gold, silver and bronze will be won by
one of these five. "
David Coleman stumbles over his numbers

> One of the great unknown champions because very little is known about him.
> **David Coleman**

"He's got to stick the boot in, to use a technical term."
Athlete Steve Ovett

"Well, Phil, tell us about your amazing third leg."
We think television presenter Ross King was discussing relays with champion runner Phil Redmond

"And there goes Juantorena down the back straight, opening his legs and showing his class."
Athletics commentator Ron Pickering

"He just can't believe what's not happening to him."
David Coleman clearly isn't seeing what is happening either

Athletics

" It's your peripheral vision that goes when
you're really exhausted; it's impossible
to see anything directly in front of you. "
**Blind panic for athlete and commentator
Sally Gunnell**

" ...and today is the night. "
**It's all as plain as day (or was it night?)
for David Coleman**

" Zola Budd – so small, so waif-like,
you literally can't see her. But there she is. "
Commentator Alan Parry

" The theme of this year's race is Robin Hood,
so here to start us off are the Three Musketeers. "
**The race announcer at the Nottingham
Marathon was gets lost in literary history**

" She went off so fast she literally died
in the last 50m. "
**Let's hope Sally Gunnell called
an ambulance, then**

" She's literally flying on a cloud! "
**Jessica Ennis's pole vault form was reaching
stratospheric heights for radio commentator
Katherine Merry**

" Linford Christie's got a habit of pulling
it out when it matters most."
David Coleman

Rose's brain will now be telling him
exactly what to do.
A no-brainer for Ron Pickering

" Marion Jones was not flying with all her
engines blazing."
Metaphors from athletics legend Steve Cram

" And I can confirm that that's the fastest time
in the world this year for Radcliffe – and she
had to do it herself."
David Coleman sees Paula is getting no help

" Marion Jones was head and feet above everyone. "
Athlete and commentator John Regis obviously looks up to the champion runner

" That was an impressive run by the two English runners – one running for England and the other for Wales. "
David Coleman might just have offended someone's national pride

" Nobody has ever won the title twice before. He [Roger Black] has already done that. "
Has he or hasn't he? David Coleman confuses us all

I think there is no doubt, she'll probably qualify for the final.
Surely David Coleman is sure?

" The girls are all very tired. They have had six big events between their legs already. "
Sally Gunnell

" Britain's last gold medal was a bronze
in 1952 in Helsinki. "

**All that glitters is not gold for commentator
Nigel Starmer-Smith**

" The reason Pinto is so far ahead is
because he is going so quickly. "

**A Homer Simpson "Doh!" moment from
athletics summariser Charlie Spedding**

Steve Ovett, Sebastian Coe, Steve Cram
– the vanguard of our cream...
Ron Pickering

" The Americans sowed the seed and
now they have reaped the whirlwind. "
Sebastian Coe

" The Republic of China – back in the
Olympic Games for the first time. "
David Coleman

" This evening is a very different evening from the morning that we had this morning. "
Sometimes David Coleman is not sure of the time of day

" That's the fastest time ever run – but it's not as fast as the world record. "
David Coleman might want to rethink this one

I'm absolutely thrilled and over the world about it.
Athlete Tessa Sanderson

" Once he'd gone past the point of no return, there was no going back. "
There was no going back for a tongue-tied BBC athletics commentator.

> He is accelerating all the time. That last lap
> was run in 64 seconds and the one before in 62.
> **David Coleman seems to be having trouble
> with his stopwatch**

" Cram nailed his colours to the mast
and threw down the Great Pretender."
Ron Pickering

" Mixed fortunes favour the brave."
David Coleman

" This is a young man who is only 25, and
you have to say, he has answered every
question that has ever been asked."
David Coleman

" Mary Decker Slaney, the world's greatest front
runner – I shouldn't be surprised to see her at
the front."
Ron Pickering

" Christie clearly has hamstring trouble, we think. "
David Coleman is hamstrung for clarity

This is a truly international field, no Britons involved.
David Coleman

" The Americans' heads are on their chins a little
bit at the moment. "
Things are a bit topsy-turvy for Ron Pickering

" I have the feeling that Machado is an athlete
who likes to get away from the opposition. "
**David Coleman reckons that athlete
Machado Manuela is a runaway success**

" She hasn't run faster than herself before. "
Athlete and commentator Zola Budd

" Born in America, John returned to his native Japan. "
**Long distance runner Mike Gratton needs
some geography lessons**

" Ingrid Kristiansen, then, has smashed the world
record, running the 5,000 metres in 14:58.89.
Truly amazing. Incidentally, this is a personal
best for Ingrid Kristiansen. "
David Coleman

" We estimate, and this isn't an estimation,
that Greta Waitz is 80 seconds behind. "
David Coleman

" And there's no 'I love you' message because
Steve Ovett has married the girl. "
**Does David Coleman have no sense
of romance?**

The Kenyans haven't done much in the last
two games, in fact they haven't competed
since 1972.
Brendan Foster

" And there you see Sebastian Coe
preparing for our first look at him. "
Jim Rosenthal

...and finally she tastes the sweet smell of success.
Ian Edwards gets his senses mixed up

" Some names to look forward to
– perhaps in the future. "
David Coleman

" The late start is due to the time. "
David Coleman

" It's a battle with himself and with
the ticking finger of the clock. "
David Coleman

" And with alphabetical irony Nigeria
follows New Zealand. "
David Coleman

" There you can see her parents. Her father died a long time ago."
Does David Coleman see ghosts?

" He's running on his nerve ends."
BBC commentator Peter West.
Ouch that must hurt

" Coe has smashed the world record – 1:44.92 has never been run easier."
Ron Pickering

" A very powerful set of lungs, very much hidden by that chest of his."
Athlete Alan Pascoe

She's not Ben Johnson, but then who is?
David Coleman

" I ran like a lemon and lemons don't run. "
A sour note for British 400m runner
Daniel Caines after a poor performance

" Moses Kiptanui, the 19-year-old Kenyan
who turned 20 a few weeks ago. "
David Coleman

" And the crowd is absolutely standing
in their seats. "
Ron Pickering

And the line-up for the final of the women's
400m hurdles includes three Russians, two
East Germans, a Pole, a Swede and a Frenchman.
Well observed by David Coleman

" He is even smaller in real life than
he is on the track. "
David Coleman

Athletics

And the mile once again becomes the focal point where it's always been.
Ron Pickering

" We keep thinking we have reached the bottom but then we find a new bottom. But I think we have reached the last bottom possible."
Amercian sprinter Michael Johnson on the Great Britain athletics team's bum performances

" He only needs to be last in this."
BBC commentator David Vine covering athletics

Ian Mackie is here to prove his back injury is behind him.
Anonymous radio commentator

He's got so much potential and most of
it still to be realised?
**Commentator Stuart Storey is waiting
for a good performance**

" [Steve] Backley must be looking forward to
the world championships, the title really could
go to anyone that's there. "
David Coleman hedging his bets

" Is there something that sticks out that
makes you an exceptional pole vaulter? "
**Television presenter Adrian Chiles deserves
some stick for this comment**

" When you go into an indoors championship
like this, it's different to the outdoors. "
Athletics coach Max Jones

" Basically, we are not human, we dropped from space like Mr Bean. Mr Bean is not a normal guy; he makes jokes. We are not normal guys. We are from space, I am from Mars. "

Sprinter Yohan Blake thinks his Jamaican team was out of this world at the 2012 Olympic Games

" Its a great advantage to be able to hurdle with both legs. "

David Coleman

Is that a grimace of pain in his right knee?

Commentator turned "medical expert" David Coleman

Boxing

Perhaps too many punches to the head is too simple an explanation for the comic bloopers from this sport, but it would certainly account for a lot! Boxers, commentators, pundits and trainers (many of them former boxers) have brought to the ring this ding-dong comic collection that really batters the senses.

Boxing

" I'm going to fade into Bolivian. "
Former heayweight champion Mike Tyson

" You can sum up this sport in two words:
'You never know.' "
**Veteran boxing trainer Lou Duva sits
on the fence about boxing**

" He's a guy who gets up at 6 a.m.
regardless of what time it is. "
Does Lou Deva know what time it is?

" I don't think you can compare like with like. "
**Boxing promoter Frank Warren reckons it's
beyond comparison**

" To be honest it was a very physical fight. "
Jim Watt

" Lennox Lewis fought the perfect fight.
He just got hit on the chin. "
**Lennox Lewis's trainer following
his fighter's shock world title defeat**

There's going to be a real ding-dong
when the bell goes.
David Coleman

" I can only see it going one way, that's my way.
How it's actually going to go I can't really say. "
British amateur boxer Nick Wilshire

" His face was a mask of blood. I think he
must have a cut somewhere. "
British boxing legend Henry Cooper

" My mum says I used to fight my way out
of the cot. But I can't remember. That was
before my time. "
Former heavyweight champion Frank Bruno

" I'm only a prawn in the game. "
British boxer Brian London

" Frank Bruno's strength, in fact, is his strength. "
Boxing commentator Reg Gutteridge

Boxing

" Born in Italy, most of his fights have been
in his native New York. "
TV presenter Des Lynam

" I would like to retire with brains still in contact. "
Boxer Herol Graham

" I'm concentrating so much I don't know
what I'm doing myself half the time. "
Former British middleweight Mark Kaylor

" I stand a 50-50 chance if not 50-60 against
anyone out there. "
**Frank Bruno needs a maths
refresher course**

" I've had 38 fights, lost one and was never
put on my feet. "
Boxing's topsy-turvy for Gary Mason

" Marvellous oriental pace he's got,
just like a Buddhist statue. "
Harry Carpenter

Boxing

" I think it was the clash of styles that made
it a good fight; we both have similar styles. "
**Perhaps a clash of heads meant Lennox
Lewis wasn't thinking straight**

Mike Tyson will have to go into a room by himself
and get used to seeing the outside world again.
Frank Bruno's thinking is inside out maybe?

" I truly believe that the confidence
I have is unbelievable. "
I believe you Prince Nazeem Hamed!

" Sure there have been injuries and deaths
in boxing – but none of them serious. "
**Former champ Alan Minter plays down
the dangers of boxing a mite too much**

" He looks up at him through
blood-smeared lips. "
Boxing commentator Harry Carpenter

Boxing

" Do I believe in superstitions? No. If you
have superstitions, that's bad luck. "
**Canadian middleweight Éric Lucas
is taking no chances**

" We'll have to take it on the chin.
It's a real body blow. "
**Anatomy isn't really British promoter
Barry Hearn's strong point**

" So over to the ringside – Harry Commentator
is your carpenter. "
BBC announcer gets tongue-tied

" I never cease to amaze myself. I say this humbly. "
**Self-effacing as ever, US boxing promoter
Don King**

" I've only ever seen Errol Christie fight once before
and that was the best I've ever seen him fight. "
Mark Kaylor

Boxing

I'll fight Lloyd Honeyghan for nothing,
if the price is right.
Marlon Starling

" This boxer is doing what's expected of him,
bleeding from the nose."
Harry Carpenter

" I had Bernard Taylor five rounds ahead
going into their fifth round."
**Former boxer turned commentator
Alan Minter**

" Pedroza, the crown on his head
hanging by a thread..."
Harry Carpenter

" No fighter comes into the ring hoping
to win – he goes in hoping to win."
Henry Cooper

Boxing

They said it would last two rounds
– they were half right, it lasted four.
Harry Carpenter

" It's not one of Bruno's fastest wins...
but it's one of them. "
Harry Carpenter isn't too sure

" Standing there making a sitting target of himself. "
Boxing manager and trainer Terry Lawless

" The Mexicans... these tiny little men
from South America... "
Harry Carpenter needs a geography lesson

" Now it comes to a simple equation:
who can stand the heat. "
Harry Carpenter

Boxing

" I don't know what impressive is,
but Joe was impressive tonight. "
**It's not hard to impress boxer
Joe Bugner's wife Marlene –
once she's grasped what it means**

" Magri has to do well against the unknown
Mexican who comes from a famous family
of five boxing brothers. "
Harry Carpenter

" Venezuela? Great! That's the Italian city
with the guys in the boats, right? "
**US boxing promoter Murad Muhammad
is a bit geographically challenged**

" We have an all-American boy here,
even though he is a Canadian. "
**National boundaries don't matter for promoter
Billy Joe Fox when talking about signing
heavyweight boxer Willie de Wit**

Cricket

The relaxed pace of the sport and the even more relaxed commentators, with hours of airtime to fill, combine to create a recipe for the occasional commentary cock-up, daft aside or hilarious double entendre. Whether uttered by Brian Johnston, Geoff Boycott, Fred Trueman or Henry Blofeld, there's never any complaint from the public as such moments have passed into cricket legend.

Cricket

" We welcome World Service listeners
to the Oval, where the bowler's Holding,
the batsman's Willey. "
**BBC cricket commentator Brian Johnston
couldn't get to grips with this**

" And umpire Dickie Bird is gestating
wildly as usual. "
**Cricket commentator Tony Lewis could
have done better with a pregnant silence**

" Brian Toss won the close. "
**Close but no prize for BBC cricket
commentator Henry Blofeld**

To stay in, you've got to not get out.
**Cricket basics simplified for the uninitiated by
former England opener Geoff Boycott**

" And the rest not only is history but will
remain history for many years to come. "
Commentator Jack Bannister

Cricket

And a sedentary seagull flies by.
It was obviously a slow day for Brian Johnston

" The lights are shining quite darkly."
**Maybe Henry Blofeld still had
his sunglasses on?**

" The crowd realises there's a match on here."
**Commentator Ravi Shastri realises
why so many people turned up for
an India v. Pakistan cricket game**

" Ray Illingworth has just relieved himself
at the Pavilion End."
Was Brian Johnston taking the piss?

" There were no scores below single figures."
**Former Australian cricket captain and
broadcaster Richie Benaud gets negative**

Cricket

" As he comes in to bowl, Freddie Titmus
has got two short legs, one of them square."
Brian Johnston

" That slow-motion replay doesn't show
how fast the ball was travelling."
**Slow motion and maybe slow wits
for Richie Benaud**

" And Ian Greig's on eight, including two fours."
England cricket legend Jim Laker

" England have no McGrathish bowlers. There
are hardly any McGrathish bowlers, except
for [Glenn] McGrath."
Stuart Law

There were congratulations and high-sixes
all round.
Richie Benaud

Cricket

" Yorkshire 332 all out, Hutton ill – I'm sorry, Hutton 111. "
Digits caused a problem for BBC newsreader John Snagge

" The Queen's Park Oval – as its name suggests, absolutely round! "
Geometry was not a strong point for West Indian cricketer Tony Cozier

" That was intentional from Gambhir. "
Cricket commentator Ravi Shastri as Gautam Gambhir hits a four

" His throw went absolutely nowhere near where it was going. "
Is this Richie Benaud's idea of a near-miss?

" England have nothing to lose here, apart from this Test match. "
Former England cricketer and coach turned commentator David Lloyd

Cricket

" I'm glad two sides of the cherry
have been put forward. "
Geoffrey Boycott

" I have prepared for the worst-case scenario,
but it could be even worse than that. "
England spin bowler Monty Panesar

" Sorry, skipper, a leopard can't change its stripes. "
Former Australian cricketer Lennie Pascoe

" We've won one on the trot. "
**Former England cricket captain
Alec Stewart appreciates a winning run**

" We have had exceptionally wet weather
in Derby – everywhere in the county
is in the same boat. "
Kenyan cricket chief Tom Sears

" Pietersen is on the charge and on the pull. "
**Is David Lloyd putting adoring ladies
on alert for the England cricketer?**

Cricket

" We didn't have metaphors in our day.
We didn't beat around the bush. "
Fred Trueman

" Unless something happens that we can't predict,
I don't think a lot will happen. "
Fred Trueman

The ball came back, literally cutting him in half.
Cricket commentator Colin Croft

" On the first day, Logie decided to chance
his arm and it came off. "
Trevor Bailey on BBC Radio

" That black cloud is coming from the direction
the wind is blowing. Now the wind is coming
from where the black cloud is. "
**Perhaps it's best that former England
captain Ray Illingworth is now a cricket
commentator and not a weatherman**

Cricket

" In Hampshire's innings the Smith
brothers scored 13 and 52 respectively. "
Henry Blofeld

" The wicket didn't do too much, but when
it did, it did too much. "
Former England captain Mike Gatting

" Michael Vaughan has a long history in
the game ahead of him. "
Cricket broadcaster Mark Nicholas

" Gul has another ball in his hand and bowls
to Bell, who has two. "
Christopher Martin-Jenkins

" This really is a fairy-book start. "
Cricketer Bob Willis

" It's a catch-21 situation. "
England batsman Kevin Pietersen

And there's the George Headley stand, named after George Headley.
South African cricket commentator Trevor Quirk

" England have a very English attack. "
Cricket commentator Geoffrey Boycott

" Gary never had a nickname – he was always called either Gary or The King. "
Cricketer Pat Pocock

" Welcome to Worcester, where you've just missed seeing Barry Richards hitting one of Basil D'Oliveira's balls clean out of the ground. "
Brian Johnston sympathises with Basil

" He's usually a good puller, but that time he couldn't get it up. "
According to Richie Benaud, someone needs Viagra

Cricket

" Laird has been brought in to stand
in the corner of the circle. "
**Richie Benaud needs to square
that circle somehow**

" Michael Atherton must think all his
Christmases are coming home at once. "
**Maybe Geoff Boycott thought
Santa Claus was next in to bat?**

" He's nearly 34 – in fact he's 33. "
Award that maths degree to Richie Benaud

" Gavin Larsen is inexperienced in Test
cricket in that this is his first Test. "
**Geoff Boycott and that first Test
problem again**

" Sean Pollock there, a carbon copy of his dad.
Except he's a bit taller and he's got red hair. "
Cricket commentator Trevor Bailey

Cricket

" There's Neil Harvey standing at leg slip with
his legs wide apart, waiting for a tickle. "
**This sort of thing is just not cricket
for Brian Johnston**

I don't think he expected it, and that's
what caught him unawares.
Trevor Bailey

" I think if you've got a safe pair of hands,
you've got a safe pair of hands. "
Cricket commentator Tom Graveney

" Anyone foolish enough to predict the
outcome of this match is a fool. "
Fred Trueman

" England might now be the favourites
to draw this match. "
Spin bowler Vic Marks seems in a spin himself

Cricket

" Mike Atherton's a thinking captain:
he gives the impression of someone
with his head on all the time. "
**Thinking is more than cricket commentator
Colin Croft was doing at the time**

" Fortunately it was a slow ball, so it wasn't
a fast one. "
Same as Geoff Boycott on this occasion?

" Now Ramprakash is facing a fish of a rather
different feather in Mark Waugh. "
**Perhaps they were flying fish for cricket
commentator Peter Baxter**

Glen McGrath bowled so badly in his
first test as though he'd never bowled in
a Test match before.
Geoff Boycott puts our brains to the test

Cricket

" Now Botham, with a chance to put everything that's gone before behind him. "
Tony Cozier

Courtney Walsh ripped the heart out of England both metaphorically and physically.
A BBC cricket commentator gets bit gory

" He seems to have had a problem with his right foot which has run with him all day. "
Could English cricketer Robin Jackman expect anything else with someone's foot?

" In Australia we have a word to describe their [Pakistan's] way of playing cricket: laissez-faire. "
An Aussie TV commentator speaks for all francophones Down Under

Cricket

" With his lovely soft hands he just tossed it off. "
Bobby Simpson observes strange goings-on at a Durham v. Lancashire match

" They're very experienced Test players with a lot of caps under them. "
Former England cricket coach Duncan Fletcher found where his players were hiding their headgear

This is the sort of pitch which literally castrates a bowler.
Is this Trevor Bailey's idea of a "no ball"?

" Strangely, in slow-motion replay, the ball seemed to hang in the air for even longer. "
Cricket commentator and former player David Acfield makes it sound like a scene from *The Matrix*

" England finally cruised to a 2-0 series win over Bangladesh through the batting of Alastair Cook, who hit a 12th Test century, and Kevin Pietersen. "

BBC Sport reporting that, despite their victory, the England players came to blows

" You almost run out of expletives for this man's fielding. "

Cricketer turned commentator Chris Broad swears by a colleague's abilities

" It's half of one, six a dozen of the other. "

Maybe Talksport commentator Chris Cowdrey's maths will improve

Once again our consistency has been proved to be inconsistent.

Cricket coach and commentator David Graveney doesn't consistently get it wrong

Cricket

It's a difficult catch to take, especially when you're running away from the ball.
Is a Sky Sports commentator accusing a cricketer of cowardice?

" Pakistan can play well, but they have the ability to play badly, too."
Cricket commentator John Embury

As the ball gets softer it loses its hardness.
Geoff Boycott stating the obvious

" If we can beat South Africa on Saturday that would be a great fillip in our cap."
Metaphorically speaking, former England captain Graham Gooch didn't have it quite right

Cricket

" He is like a guardsman; every part of him erect. "
Was BBC's cricket legend Henry Blofeld
talking about stiff opposition?

Dean Hadley has left the field with a back injury;
more news on that as soon as it breaks.
Fractured logic from BBC cricket correspondent
Pat Murphy

" Zimbabwe have done well, just as it looked as
though the horse had left the stable and gone
galloping down the road, they managed to
put a chain on the door. "
Cricket commentator Peter Baxter rides
in with some horsey metaphors

" You can't get any earlier than the second
ball of the game. "
Obviously the first ball doesn't count
for commentator David Lloyd

Cricket

" And this game is coming nicely to a climax;
like a well-cooked Welsh rabbit. "
**A BBC Radio 4 commentator gives
it plenty of bunny**

" You've got to make split-second decisions
so quickly. "
**Geoff Boycott's mouth was a split-second
ahead of his brain**

" The only person who could be better than
Brian Lara could be Brian Lara himself. "
Colin Croft obviously rates Brian Lara

" Jack Russell may be the artist but Metson showed
he's a rhyming couplet of a wicketkeeper. "
**A BBC radio cricket report that
was pure poetry**

" It was all so easy for Walsh. All he had to do was
drop an arm and there it was, on the ground. "
Cricket commentator Tony Lewis

Cricket

He has got perfect control over the ball right up to the minute he lets it go.
Cricket correspondent Peter Walker

" I presented my trousers to the committee; I had nothing to hide. "
Hope England cricket captain Mike Atherton kept his boxer shorts on, though?

" They've sent Shah in at three. It's a good move, it'll give him time to play himself in before he explodes. "
Commentator Harsha Bhogle

" We decided to put the foot on the pedal towards the end – and it came off. "
English cricketer Paul Collingwood

" That was a good catch from Matsikenyeri, running away from himself. "
A Sky Sports commentator lacking direction

Cricket

" People have to realise we're the only
northern hemisphere team in cricket. "
**Paul Collingwood needs reminding that the
West Indies, India, Pakistan, Sri Lanka and
Bangladesh are also in the northern hemisphere**

Yes, he's a very good cricketer – pity he's not
a better batter or bowler.
Former English cricketer Tom Graveney

" The Queen's Park Oval, exactly as its name
suggests, is absolutely round. "
Geometry wasn't Tony Crozier's strong point

" I don't think I've ever seen anything quite like that
before – it's the second time it's happened today. "
Déjà vu for BBC commentator Brian Johnston

Cricket

"Ah yes, sledging. In the days before microphones on the pitch, we got that blind MP chap up into the commentary box to lip read."
BBC cricket commentator Brian Johnston swears by the old methods

"Jon Lewis is a real Essex boy… born in Isleworth, Middlesex."
BBC cricket summariser Tony Lewis has a problem with geography

Defreitas… just in the back of his mind he is wearing a support.
It's a good job Geoffrey Boycott took up cricket and not anatomy

Football

The world's most popular sport has made a telling contribution to sports commentary calamities. Whether it is the confused cliché, the mixed metaphor or the stating of the blindingly obvious, few sports can compare. With so many comic offerings from commentators, aided and abetted by managers and players, it is often rarer for a person to talk sense than to say something daft!

Football

" Someone in the England team will
have to grab the ball by the horns. "
**Doesn't TV soccer pundit and former manager
Ron Atkinson know about the handball rule?**

" I've told you a million times, I don't exaggerate. "
Former Arsenal striker Charlie Nicholas

" Nethercott is literally standing
in Le Tissier's pocket. "
**BBC pundit David Pleat sees some strange
things in an English football match**

Sporting Lisbon in their green and white hoops,
looking like a team of zebras.
**Clearly BBC sports reporter Peter Jones
hasn't been to the zoo lately**

Football

" Forest have now lost six matches without winning. "
David Coleman

Goalkeepers aren't born today
until they're in their late 20s or 30s.
**That's some gestation period according
to former player and manager Kevin Keegan**

" In some ways, cramp is worse than
having a broken leg. "
**Not sure doctors would agree with
Kevin Keegan's diagnosis**

" Gary always weighed up his options,
especially when he had no choice. "
Kevin Keegan

" You can see the ball go past them, or the man, but you'll never see both man and ball go past at the same time. So if the ball goes past, the man won't, or if the man goes past, they'll take the ball. "

Ron Atkinson... and his point was?

" Fulham needed that three points because they were slowly sinking to the bottom of the table very, very quickly. "

Pundit Mark Lawrenson is no judge of speed

" He's been one of the best centre backs/full backs for the past 12 decades. "

Liverpool's Jamie Carragher has had a very long-playing career according to fellow player Michael Owen

" Brooking trying one of those impossible crosses, which on that occasion was impossible. "

Brian Moore

When Paul Scholes gets it [tackling] wrong, they come in so late that they arrive yesterday.
Time travel for Ron Atkinson

" Emile Zola has scored again for Chelsea."
**A BBC Radio 5 Live commentator
sees the literary side of a football match**

" If you expose the opposition's weaknesses enough, then, in the end, those weaknesses will be exposed."
Football manager Sam Allardyce

" This will be their 19th consecutive game without a win unless they can get an equaliser."
BBC football reporter Alan Green

" Martin O'Neill, standing, hands on hips, stroking his chin."
Do BBC sports reporter Mike Ingham's eyes deceive him?

It's now 1–1, an exact reversal of the score line on Saturday.
Radio 5 Live

" The Uruguayans are losing no time in making a meal around the referee. "
This match was no picnic for Mike Ingham

" Poland 0, England 0, though England are now looking the better value for their nil. "
Nil points for the logic of BBC sports commentator Barry Davies

" Arsenal shouldn't be too concerned, because every team has a bit of a blip during the season. Last year they had one. "
Football's Ray Wilkins

" I would advise anyone coming to the match to come early and not to leave until the end, otherwise they might miss something. "
Football pundit John Toshack

" Peru score their third, and it's 3-1 to Scotland. "
**There's that old maths problem again for
David Coleman**

" If that had gone in, it would have been a goal. "
David Coleman

Ian Rush is deadly 10 times out of 10,
but that wasn't one of them.
3 out of 10 on commentary for Peter Jones

" Neil Sullivan has stopped absolutely
everything thrown at him...
Wimbledon 1, Manchester United 1. "
Football commentator Mike Ingham

" And there'll be more football in a moment,
but first we've got the highlights of the
Scottish League Cup Final. "
BBC sports reporter Gary Newbon

Football

" Petr Cech will want a clean sheet having been unusually leaky in the past few weeks. "
Match of the Day **commentator gets personal about the Chelsea goalkeeper**

This chance is unmissable and well, er, he misses it!
Pundit Alan Hansen seems miss-tified

" After that (the Simon Davies goal), you just could smell it – Hamburg got very nervous. "
Summariser Chris Coleman can sniff out a victory

" Julian Dicks is everywhere. It's like they've got eleven Dicks on the field. "
Britain's Metro Radio commentator makes a dick of himself

Football

" For me their biggest threat is when they
get into the attacking part of the field. "
Ron Atkinson gets down to the ethos of football

" If you score against the Italians you deserve a goal. "
Ron Atkinson

" Football's football: if that weren't the
case it wouldn't be the game that it is. "
So said the BBC's Garth Crooks

" Steven Gerrard makes runs into the box
better than anyone. So does Frank Lampard. "
**Former Premier League player and commentator
Jamie Redknapp**

Sometimes in football you have to score goals.
**Even if you resort to using your hands, according
to French footballer Thierry Henry**

Football

" Portuguese international singer Cristiano Ronaldo has signed a two-year extension to his contract. "
The CNN online football report announces a change of career for the player

" I would love to be able to get to the stage where things are all rosy in the garden. But I am not yet looking at pastures new, although right now we have given the critics a field day. "
Football manager Alex McLeish gets all horticultural

" One accusation you can't throw at me is that I've always done my best. "
Footballer Cristiano Ronaldo can bamboozle with this feet – or his mouth.

" Henchoz advanced to the halfway line and exposed himself. "
Former footballer and summariser Graeme Le Saux was on to that in a flash

> Well, Real Madrid might have got the points, but it was an unconvincing 1-0 draw.
> **Sky Sport's Rob Palmer makes it far from clear**

" We lost because we didn't win. "
Could the lager be responsible for Sweden football manager Lars Lagerback getting tongue-tied?

" I always want to play for my country. I'm here if they need me for the rest of my life, and hopefully after that as well. "
Brazil's Romario is in heaven about playing for the national side

" It's difficult to find a defect on Mourinho, perhaps he is a little introverted but he is marvellous. "
Inter Milan president Massimo Moratti is not too sure about coach Jose Mourinho!

Football

" I would not be bothered if we lost every game
as long as we won the World Cup. "
**German football star Michael Ballack
clearly hadn't thought this through**

" West Germany's Briegel hasn't been able
to get past anyone yet – that's his trademark. "
BBC sports reporter John Helm

" You don't score 64 goals in 86 games
without being able to score goals. "
**BBC sports reporter Alan Green
is quite right**

It's headed away by John Clark, using his head.
**Football commentator Derek Rae clearly
wasn't using his, though**

And with just four minutes gone,
the score is already 0–0.
**Impressive deduction from
BBC sports reporter Ian Darke**

" The USA are a goal down, and if
they don't get a goal they'll lose. "
John Helm

" And Bale slides the ball inside Cech. "
**John Motson sees a painful pass from
Spurs' winger Gareth Bale**

" He dribbles a lot and opposition doesn't
like it – you can see it all over their faces. "
Ron Atkinson

" Celtic manager Davie Hay still has
a fresh pair of legs up his sleeve. "
Football pundit John Greig

Football

" At half-time Ardiles said go out there
and throw the kitchen sink at them.
Spurs are doing that, literally. "
**Doesn't former footballer Alan Mullery know
that sink throwing is a red-card offence?**

" McCarthy shakes his head in agreement
with the referee. "
Body language is not Martin Tyler's strong point

" It was the game that put the Everton ship
back on the road. "
BBC sports reporter Alan Green

The ageless Dennis Wise, now in his 30s.
Martin Tyler

" We haven't had the rub of the dice. "
Bobby Robson

" I'd love to be a mole on the wall in
the Liverpool dressing room at half-time."
Kevin Keegan

Footballers are no different from human beings.
Former England manager Graham Taylor

" I couldn't settle in Italy – it was like
living in a foreign country."
**Liverpool legend Ian Rush on his
spell at Juventus**

" I want to win the Nobel Peace Prize – and I'm
going to fight as hard as I can to make it happen."
Brazil football star Ronaldo

Football

" Even when you're dead you shouldn't lie down and let yourself be buried. "
Football manager Gordon Lee

" It's the end-of-season curtain-raiser. "
Former Aston Villa striker Peter Withe

" I'd like to have seen Tony Morley left on as a down-and-out winger. "
Blackpool legend and football commentator Jimmy Armfield

" ...and their manager, Terry Neil, isn't here today, which suggests he is elsewhere. "
Football commentator Brian Moore

" I'm not going to make it a target but it is something to aim for. "
Ex-Manchester United star Steve Coppell

" The Spaniards have been reduced to aiming aimless balls into the box. "
Ron Atkinson

A few question marks are being asked
of the Honduran defence.
Alan Green

" I think if they hadn't scored, we might
have got a better result. "
**Former Leeds United manager
Howard Wilkinson**

" The last player to score a hat-trick in a cup
final was Stan Mortenson. He even had a
final named after him – the Matthews final. "
**Football history is not a strong point for
former manager Lawrie McMenemy**

" He's got his hands on his knees and holds
his head in despair. "
Peter Jones

" If you stand still there is only one way to go,
and that's backwards. "
England goalkeeping legend Peter Shilton

Football

" I had a lump in my mouth as the ball went in. "
Former England manager Terry Venables

" Wenger is still sweating on Sol Campbell's hamstring. "
Is Arsenal's website giving away medical secrets?

" Some of these players never dreamed they'd be playing in a cup final at Wembley – but here they are today, fulfilling those dreams. "
Lawrie McMenemy

" And Ritchie has now scored 11 goals, exactly double the number he scored last season. "
BBC sports reporter Alan Parry

" So different from the scenes in 1872, at the FA Cup that none of us can remember. "
BBC football commentator John Motson

" They can beat anybody on the day, but they can also lose against anybody on the day. "
Former Liverpool football star Emlyn Hughes

Football

" Real possession football this. And Zico's lost it. "
John Helm

" It's a game of two teams. "
BBC football reporter Peter Brackley

" Well, we got nine and you can't score
more than that. "
**Former England football manager
Bobby Robson**

" Queen's Park against Forfar – you can't get more
romantic than that. "
Archie McPherson

" With the last kick of the game,
Bobby McDonald scored with a header. "
Alan Parry

" I am a firm believer that if you score one goal
the other team have to score two to win. "
Howard Wilkinson

Football

" Football's a game of skill; we kicked them a bit and they kicked us a bit. "
Former England football hard man Graham Roberts

" There's a one-man Liverpool wall, hurriedly put together. "
Football commentator John Murray

" Kicked wide of the goal with such precision. "
Des Lynam

" If you're 0–0 down, there's no one better to get you back on terms than Michael Owen. "
Former player and match summariser Andy Townsend

There are a whole lot of teams in the bottom six this season.
Graeme Le Saux

A run of 24 games without defeat must be a millstone on your shoulders.
Reverse thinking here from the BBC's Tony Gubba

" I'd like to think it's a case of crossing the i's and dotting the t's. "
Former manager Dave Bassett

" I never predict anything and I never will do. "
Footballer Paul Gascoigne is predictable

" I want more from David Beckham. I want him to improve on perfection. "
Kevin Keegan was quite demanding as England football manager

" For those of you watching in black and white, Spurs are playing in yellow. "
John Motson

Marseille needed to score first, and that never looked likely once Liverpool had taken the lead.
David Pleat

" They're the second-best team in the world and there's no higher praise than that."
Kevin Keegan

" You can't do better than go away from home and get a draw."
Kevin Keegan reckons without the possibility of a win

" Well, let's say there's no place like Wembley for the winners and there certainly isn't for the runners-up."
BBC commentator

Football

" I saw him kick the bucket over there which suggests he's not going to be able to continue."
Football pundit Trevor Brooking

" Hamburg are the European champions!"
**ITV football commentator Brian Moore
immediately after the final whistle of
the 1980 European Cup final which
Nottingham Forest had won 1–0**

" I'm not going to pick out anyone in particular,
but Jay Jay Okocha should not be captain
of a football club."
Former footballer Rodney Marsh

Goodnight, and don't forget to put your
cocks back.
Football pundit Jimmy Hill

" I never comment on referees and I'm not going to break the habit of a lifetime for that prat. "
Ron Atkinson lets fly at officialdom

He's shown a lack of inconsistency.
Former Premier League manager Chris Coleman

Interviewer: "Teko, what's your favourite food?"
Teko: "It's hard, but I'm going to have to say breakfast."
Orlando Pirates midfielder Teko Modise

" If ever a goal ever needed a game, this is it. "
Former footballer Tony Gale

" Fire and broomstick. "
Football pundit David O'Leary

> Well, I've seen some tackles, Jonathan,
> but that was the ultimatum!
> **Alan Mullery**

" Jurgen Klinsmann, who refutes
to earn £25,000 a week..."
**Alan Mullery reckons Klinsmann is in denial
about his pay deal**

" He's not going to adhere himself to the fans."
Another malapropism from Alan Mullery

" It doesn't endow me, to be honest."
Alan Mullery

" I can't understand the notoriety of people."
Alan Mullery

Football

Alan Brazil: "Will he be doing any commentaries for us during the World Cup?"
Co-commentator: "Well not unless he's going to be doing them from the grave, Alan."

" Our talking point this morning is George Best, his liver transplant and the booze culture in football. Don't forget, the best caller wins a crate of John Smith's."
Alan Brazil

" Our central defenders, Doherty and Anthony Gardner, were fantastic and I told them that when they go to bed tonight they should think of each other."
David Pleat

The man [Sir Alex Ferguson] is United through and through – cut him and he bleeds red."
So presumably would Alan Brazil, too

Football

" I've told the players we need to win so that
I can have the cash to buy some new ones. "
**Football manager Chris Turner has a
strange idea of player-motivation techniques**

" Never go for a 50–50 ball
unless you are 80–20 sure. "
BBC football correspondent Ian Dark

" If we played like that every week
we wouldn't be so inconsistent. "
**Former Manchester United player
Bryan Robson**

" It's hard to be passionate twice a week. "
**George Graham on Arsenal's
punishing schedule**

" And there's Ray Clemence looking
as cool as ever out in the cold. "
Jimmy Hill

" That's football, Mike. Northern Ireland
have had several chances and haven't scored but
England had no chances and scored twice. "
Trevor Brooking

" The Arsenal defence is skating close
to the wind. "
**Obviously a cold wind for football
pundit Jack Charlton**

" And sitting on the Watford bench is Ernie
Whalley's brother Tom. Both Welshman. "
Brian Moore

" They've flown in from all over the world,
so have the rest of the world team. "
Brian Moore

Brian Butler: "Did you ever have any doubts
about yourself when you left Tottenham?"
Peter Shreeve: "I don't think so."

Celtic were at one time nine points ahead, but somewhere along the road, their ship went off the rails.

Football reporter Richard Park seems all at sea

" That's Robson – a total convicted player. "
Jimmy Armfield

" Peter Reid is hobbling, and I've got a feeling that will slow him down. "
John Motson

" If we get promotion, let's sit down and see where we stand. "
Football manager Roy McFarland

" You've got to miss them to score sometimes. "
Football manager Dave Bassett

" This is the first time Denmark has ever reached the World Cup Finals, so this is the most significant moment in Danish history. "
Would the people of Denmark agree with John Helm?

" The World Cup – truly an international event. "
John Motson

" Nearly all the Brazilian supporters are wearing yellow shirts – it's a fabulous kaleidoscope of colour! "
Colour is not John Motson's strongpoint

" I don't know why Glenn Murray took the penalty. I suppose because he is our penalty taker. "
Brighton Albion manager Gus Poyet

Paul Gascoigne has recently become a father and been booked for over-celebrating.
John Motson

That's an old Ipswich move – O'Callaghan crossing for Mariner to drive over the bar.
John Motson

" Brazil – they're so good it's like they are running around the pitch playing with themselves. "
John Motson

" Unfortunately, we keep kicking ourselves in the foot. "
It's painful for footballer Ray Wilkins

" I would not say he [David Ginola] is the best left winger in the Premiership, but there are none better. "
Ron Atkinson

" An inch or two either side of the post and that would have been a goal. "
Dave Bassett speaking on Sky Sports

Football

" Both sides have scored a couple of goals, and both sides have conceded a couple of goals."
Peter Withe, speaking on Radio 5 Live

" The most vulnerable area for goalies is between their legs..."
Commentator Andy Gray

" The lad got over excited when he saw the whites of the goalpost's eyes."
Steve Coppell, BBC Radio 5 Live

" If you can't stand the heat in the dressing room, get out of the kitchen."
What's cooking for Terry Venables?

" ...but Arsenal are quick to credit Bergkamp with laying on 75 per cent of their nine goals."
Tony Gubba

" Beckenbauer really has gambled all his eggs."
Ron Atkinson

" We threw our dice into the ring
and turned up trumps."
**Pundit Bruce Rioch reckons
football's a gamble**

...and the news from Guadalajara where the
temperature is 96 degrees, is that Falcao is
warming up.
Brian Moore

" If history is going to repeat itself I should
think we can expect the same thing again."
Terry Venables

" I'm not a believer in luck...
but I do believe you need it."
Former England footballer Alan Ball

" I think that was a moment of cool panic there."
Ron Atkinson

Football

" I spent four indifferent years at Goodison Park,
but they were great years. "
Former goalkeeper Martin Hodge

" Souness gave Fleck a second chance and
he grabbed it with both feet. "
Journalist James Sanderson

" They have missed so many chances they
must be wringing their heads in shame. "
Former England manager Ron Greenwood

" Dumbarton player Steve McCahill has
limped off with a badly cut forehead. "
Scottish radio journalist Tom Ferrie

A contract on a piece of paper, saying you
want to leave, is like a piece of paper
saying you want to leave.
Former Chelsea manager John Hollins

" And I honestly believe we can go all the way to Wembley – unless somebody knocks us out. "
Dave Bassett

" In terms of the Richter Scale this defeat was a force eight gale. "
Former West Ham United manager John Lyall

In comparison, there's no comparison.
Ron Greenwood

" I would also think that the action replay showed it to be worse than it actually was. "
Ron Atkinson

" Mirandinha will have more shots this afternoon than both sides put together. "
Newcastle United legend Malcolm Macdonald

" Newcastle, of course, unbeaten in their last five wins. "
Brian Moore

" Certain people are for me and certain
people are pro me. "
Terry Venables

" What I said to them at half-time would be
unprintable on the radio. "
Former Tottenham manager Gerry Francis

John Harkes going to Sheffield, Wednesday.
New York Post

" If there weren't such a thing as football,
we'd all be frustrated footballers. "
Former Everton captain Mick Lyons

" The crowd think that Todd handled the ball. They
must have seen something that nobody else did. "
Barry Davies

Football

" I can see the carrot at the end of the tunnel. "
England legend Stuart Pearce

They compare Steve McManaman to
Steve Heighway and he's nothing like
him, but I can see why – it's because
he's a bit different.
Kevin Keegan

" Glenn Hoddle hasn't been the Hoddle
we know. Neither has Bryan Robson. "
Ron Greenwood

" There's no way Ryan Giggs is another
George Best. He's another Ryan Giggs. "
Scottish legend Denis Law

" I don't think there is anybody bigger
or smaller than Maradona. "
Kevin Keegan

Jimmy Hill: "Don't sit on the fence, Terry, what chance do you think Germany has got of getting through?"
Terry Venables: "I think it's 50-50."

" They didn't change positions, they just moved the players around."
Terry Venables

" What disappointed me was that we didn't play with any passion. I'm not disappointed, you know, I'm just disappointed."
Kevin Keegan

" They had to get the brassieres to thaw it out."
Ken Jones discussing a frozen pitch

" If Glenn Hoddle said one word to his team at half-time, it was concentration and focus."
Ron Atkinson

Football

" 80 per cent of teams who score first in matches go on to win them. But they may draw some – or occasionally lose."
David Pleat

" I'd like to play for an Italian club, like Barcelona."
Former Aston Villa midfielder Mark Draper needs to grab an atlas

" The referee looks at his whistle."
Football commentator Dave Woods

" Well, Harry, fifth place last year, how can you better that?"
Fergus Sweeney

Macclesfield have come out in the second half with all guns steaming.
Hot air in the commentary box from Brian Seymour-Smith

Football

Commentator 1: "Looks like he's pulled his groin and has to come off."
Commentator 2: "Yeah, he must have done it during the one or two touches he's had in this game..."
Two BBC commentators debating how Liverpool's Maxi Rodriguez got his injury

" Today was about our lack of ability to not produce the ability that we've got. "
Hope West Ham manager Sam Allardyce's team talks are more clear cut

" I look forward to hearing from the silent majority. "
Former manager turned pundit Alex McLeish is listening carefully

" In the papers this morning; 'police closing in on Ian Holloway'. Sorry 'Palace closing in on Ian Holloway. "
Football pundit Alan Brazil

Football

" I haven't seen it, but it looks generous. "
Arsenal manager Arsene Wenger seems psychic

The title race is between two horses and a little horse that needs milk and needs to learn how to jump. Maybe next season we can race.
Chelsea manager Jose Mourinho on Chelsea's title credentials

" I've been consistent in patches this season. "
Arsenal player Theo Walcott is not sure about himself.

" He's been like a fresh of breath air. "
Manchester United legend turned pundit Roy Keane

" It's nice for us to have a fresh face in the camp to bounce things off. "
Football manager Lawrie Sanchez

" Berbatov put the penalty away like he was
putting a penalty away."
Chris Kamara is definite about the penalty

" Paolo Di Canio is one picnic short of a hamper."
Alan Brazil

" Whoever you support, you've got that blood
in your veins."
Former player Phil Neal's bloody right

In the end, Rosicky initially did well.
Andy Townsend gets a little mixed up

" Paolo di Cano managed with a bar of iron."
Former Arsenal midfilelder Paul Merson

" I think Southampton will finish above teams
that are well below them."
Paul Merson again

Football

" He could see the whites of the goals."
Former Liverpool player Jamie Redknapp
gets his metaphors in a twist

" Arsenal needed to get a result at White Hart Lane
like they did last year, albeit they were at home."
Sky Sport's Redknapp strikes again

" I managed lots of clubs. I had more
clubs than Jack Nicholson."
Former player and manager Bobby Gould
has a new take on the old Tommy Docherty
quote but fails to get it right

" This is a once in a lifetime opportunity,
but at least we've got another game on Tuesday."
Marvin Sordell's inopportune comment

" There is no precedent for what Suarez did,
other than he's done it before."
An unprecedented comment from pundit
and ex-player Danny Mills

" One or two Scotland players have got
to look themselves in the face. "
**Alan Brazil will get his fellow countrymen
seeing double**

It's turning into a war of nutrition in midfield.
**Food for thought from ex-Arsenal star
Martin Keown.**

" Sandro's holding his face. You can tell
from that it's a knee injury. "
**You can tell Dion Dublin was a footballer
and not a doctor**

" Brendan Rodgers has been singing the praises
of Suarez and Sturridge – the SS. "
Perhaps Alan Brazil shouldn't mention the war

" Sir Alex is going to be such a big, big,
big hole to replace. "
Steve Bruce voids Ferguson's career

Football

" Phil Dowd checks his whistle
and blows his watches."
Commentator Alan Green

" He was a quiet man, Eric Cantona,
but he was a man of few words."
**David Beckham should have been
a man of fewer words here**

" Giroud scored with a brilliant header
with the last kick of the game."
Chris Kamara doesn't know his feet from his head

" Great teams always have a Plan B. Look at
Barcelona. Their Plan B is to stick to Plan A."
Pundit Johnny Giles had no verbal Plan B either

His brother-in-law is Scott Parker,
so he's got a good pedigree.
David Pleat mucks up a family tree

After Chelsea scored, Bolton epitulated.
Paul Merson has a verbal capitulation on air

" Football's not just physical, it's menthol too. "
**Southend United manager Phil Brown's
comment is worth a mint**

" Arsenal literally finished the game after
15 minutes. "
Former Arsenal striker Ian Wright

" Javier Chevanton don't speak the language
too good. "
Neither does ex-player and manager Kevin Bond

" Does Di Canio look like Jimmy Nesbitt, or is it
Jimmy Nesbitt who looks like Di Canio? "
Mick Quinn's identity crisis

" Aaron Ramsey hasn't always been the flavour
of the Arsenal fans' eyes. "
Radio summariser Craig Burley

Football

" I can never predict my future because a
big part of my future is already behind me. "
**Back to the future for ex-Chelsea boss
Guus Hiddink**

" Benitez took the elephant in the room
and put it on the table. "
Pundit Gareth Southgate

" There's been a lot of pavola about that whole
Beckham thing... "
Brian Kerr makes a right palaver of this comment

" Scoring goals is the hardest thing in football but
doing it in a struggling team is even harder. "
Paul Merson states the obvious

Usmanov has got loads of money – we know
that from his wealth.
**Darren Gough is counting the cost
of this piece of silliness**

Football

" If that happens anywhere else on the pitch,
it's a stonewall penalty. "
**Does Chris Kamara need a refresher
course on the rules of the game?**

" It was a no-needful tackle from Danny Fox. "
Manchester United's Phil Neville needs a dictionary

" If QPR go into the Championship, the players
will be like rats jumping over a ship. "
**Mick Quinn watches out for high-flying
rodents at Loftus Road**

" Wes Brown stepped into the plate today. "
Niall Quinn sees some crockery on the pitch

It can only happen in football – it's the
Rocky Balboa scenario.
**Ex-West Ham manager Alvin Martin
mixes his sports and his metaphors**

" You need to take off your rose-scented glasses. "
**Smells like a comment from BBC pundit
Robbie Savage**

" There are fractions within the Manchester
City dressing room. "
Danny Mills tells only a part of the story

Only one thing can stop Luis Suarez from
being voted as the Players' Player of the Year
– his fellow players.
Jamie Redknapp states the obvious.

" You have to put your shoes in
Daniel Levy's shoes. "
Mick Quinn is in a tight spot

" Ricky Lambert's brain is very clever. "
Paul Merson

> For me, Loic Remy is the key to this goal.
> **Strangely Jamie Redknapp had it right because Remy had scored**

" Berahino hasn't been the best player on the pitch but he's my man of the match. "
Owen Hargreaves doesn't quite understand the concept of man of the match

" Sometimes you've got to swallow the bullet. "
Ex-player Brian Little shoots himself in the foot with a metaphor

" It was handbags at half-mast. "
Newcastle manager Alan Pardew had better not tell the Royal Navy.

" Tony Fernandes is in that goldfish bowl and he's swimming against the tide. "
Former player Niall Quinn is talking wet

Football

" That's a yellow card for Cazorla. So the next time
he's involved in Europe, he won't be."
George Hamilton loses his normal verbal agility

" Wilshere looks like he's got the grit
between his teeth."
**BBC's Darren Gough leaves a nasty taste
in the Arsenal midfielder's mouth**

" Swansea are in cloud dreamland."
Clarke Carlisle has his head in the clouds

" It's all pumps blazing as we go to the wire."
**Too many metaphors can be
David Pleat's downfall**

There's no such thing as a must-win game,
and this is one of them.
Former player Alan Wright gets tongue-tied

" We couldn't defend a fish supper."
**Sam Allardyce chips in with a
comment about his team**

Gareth Bale has been levitated to the status
of one of the best players in the world.
Perry Groves reckons Bale is a high flier.

" Any side in the world would miss Bareth Gale."
David Pleat finds Gareth Bale a tongue twister.

" It was six of a half and one dozen of the other."
Danny Higginbotham

" I think the next United manager is already
at the club. It could be either Ryan Giggs or
Ole Gunnar Solksjaer, who isn't at the club."
Michael Gray

" It's great to get that duck off my back."
Chelsea and England's Gary Cahill

Sidwell, Parker and Duff are all coming back
to pastures old, as the saying goes.
Stan Collymore puts an old slant on an old adage

" Big Sam has played his last dice. "
Chris Kamara is a real card when it comes to gaffes

" N'Zonzi... so cool there, he didn't batter
an eyelid. "
Commentator Gareth Owen

" If he scores, it's a different kettle of story. "
Adrian Chiles was trying to speak metaphorically

" Villa were playing against defenders with
no confidence, then they took whatever
confidence they had left. "
Kevin Keegan was quite confident about that

" Muller is non-stop perpetual motion. "
**Former player Graeme Souness is non-stop
on superlatives**

" The aura of uninvincibility has gone,
if there is such a word. "
**Someone give television presenter
Adrian Chiles a dictionary**

" I got a text from my daughter saying
she was having contraptions. "
**Peterborough boss Barry Fry gets tongue
tied over becoming a granddad**

Whatever happened to Dagenham and Redgrave?
**Alan Brazil needs telling it's Dagenham and
Redbridge**

" Who'll win the league? It's a coin toss between
three of them. "
Ex-Southampton star Matt Le Tissier

" Karl Henry's got himself sent off for
a deliberate red card. "
Chris Kamara needs sending off for this one

Football

" Are Spurs title contenders for the league?"
Mick Quinn poses a difficult question

" The possession stats at one point were
77 per cent to 33 per cent."
**Mick Quinn always gives 110% in his
summarizing**

" What I saw in Holland and Germany was
that the majority of people are Dutch in Holland
and German in Germany."
Manager Peter Taylor gets a lesson in nationhood

" In the last year, 46 of the 92 managers have lost
their jobs – that's over half."
Nearly, David Pleat, nearly

" A game is not won until it is lost."
You can't argue with David Pleat on this one

" I saw a defeat coming when they went 3-0 down."
David Pleat didn't need a crystal ball

" His ability was natural and that's what you call natural ability. "
Kevin Keegan is right, naturally

" Tottenham have lost all their European quarter finals since they last won one. "
Commentator Clive Tyldesley

The Villa keeper, Brad Goujon…
Mick Quinn reckons Brad Guzan is tasty

" Manchester City are going to go and win the Premier League this year, as long as they can get their complacency right. "
Paul Merson

" West Brom haven't got the money to leave people roasting in the reserves. "
Competition for places is hot at the Baggies according to Paul Merson

Football

" I came in 11 years ago. I remember
it like it was tomorrow. "
**Time stood still for David Moyes when
he was Everton's manager**

" Sometimes he does the brilliant things really well. "
Ex-Manchester United player Lee Sharpe

" Frank Lampard has still got the same legs
he had five years ago. "
**No leg transplants for the Chelsea man as far as
coach Ray Wilkins can see**

" Tony Adams is braised for rejection by Arsenal. "
Alan Brazil sees the centre back done to a turn

If you don't give Martinez a chance,
what chance has he got?
Paul Merson

Football

" Sir Alex Ferguson is tough shoes to follow. "
Mick Quinn puts his foot in it

" We were not good enough today, particularly
in the fringe department. "
**Sam Allardyce gives his team
a hair-dressing down**

" You often see shocks in the League Cup, even
when you don't expect them. "
Commentator and ex-Liverpool player Jan Molby

" Aston Villa have literally metaphorically had their
pants pulled down. "
Dion Dublin talking total pants

" Manchester City have got the best, if not the
second-best, squad in the league. "
Georgie Bingham just cannot make up his mind

" Sir Alex is going to continue to keep going. "
Tautology from Manchester United's Gary Neville

" Arsenal's width comes from wide areas. "
Jamie Redknapp is spaced out?

It falls to the ageless 35-year-old Frank Lampard.
**Does George Hamilton think
Lampard is Methuselah?**

" I don't want Rooney to leave these shores
but if he does, I think he'll go abroad. "
Ian Wright

" Stokes gets a straight yellow for that challenge. "
Ronnie Whelan is a real card

" If that ball had dropped to a West Brom
player who'd put it in the net, that would
have been the equalizer. "
**Trevor Francis should know as
he was a lethal striker in his playing days**

" Sessegnon gets it on his left-hand foot. "
Is Iain Dowie watching handball or football?

So, Romelu Lukaku, you speak six languages.
Which ones? Obviously, there's Belgian...
**Commentator Pat Murphy fails even to get one
out of the six as, in Lukaku's Belgian homeland,
the languages are Flemish and French**

" These are players that are trying to put food
in the manager's head. "
Ex-player Jason McAteer gives food for thought

" We have a number of two-footed players in this
country at the moment – Morrison, Barkley and
Townsend – and they are unique. "
Just as Jamie Redknapp's many gaffes are unique

" We didn't underestimate them. They were just a lot better than we thought. "
England manager Bobby Robson, after the 1990 World Cup game against Cameroon

Mark Hughes at his very best: he loves to feel people right behind him.
Kevin Keegan

" I'm going to make a prediction; it could go either way. "
Ron Atkinson sitting on the fence

" My parents have been there for me, ever since I was about seven. "
David Beckham

" The new West Stand casts a giant shadow over the entire pitch, even on a sunny day. "
Chris Jones seems in the dark

Golf

Perhaps it is the lush greens or the clubhouse ambience, but few broadcasters get caught up in the moment as much as golf commentators. Their need to describe the beautiful setting or the moment of extreme golfing tension often means they have tendency to state – to our amusement – the seemingly obvious. Add to this commentary hazards of the golfing lexicon – "birdie", "hole" and "69" – and you have a full round of hilarious sports slip-ups.

He [Ernie Els] has just got engaged which is perhaps why he produced a 69 today.
Is BBC golf correspondent Tony Adamson getting a bit personal?

" As the cock crows, it's only about 200 yards. "
Golf commentator Peter Alliss

" A very small crowd here today. I can count the people on one hand. Can't be more than 30. "
Perhaps Michael Abrahamson has big hands?

" One of the reasons Arnie Palmer is playing so well is that, before each final round, his wife takes out his balls and kisses them. Oh, my God, what have I just said? "
An unnamed US Open TV commentator will never live this one down

Golf

" And now to hole eight, which is
in fact the eighth hole. "
Peter Alliss

" That was a beautiful shot.
Inch perfect – but an inch wide. "
**A BBC golf commentator just wasn't
measuring up on the day**

" Some weeks Nick likes to use Fanny;
other weeks he prefers to do it by himself. "
**Ken Brown talking about golfer
Nick Faldo's caddy Fanny Sunesson –
from a sporting point of view, of course**

Pinero has missed the putt. I wonder
what he's thinking in Spanish.
**BBC commentator Renton Laidlaw
wonders what "Oh, bugger" is in Spanish**

There he stands with his legs akimbo.
**Surely golf pundit Peter Alliss is
pulling someone's leg?**

" Sandy Lyle talking to Tony Adamson,
a lifetime ambition fulfilled."
BBC commentator Ian Robertson

" I think Steve is the nicest guy in the world,
too, so it couldn't happen to a nicer guy."
**Luke Donald is convinced about
how nice Steve Stricker is**

Peter Alliss: "What do you think
of the climax of this tournament?"
Peter Thomson: "I'm speechless."
Alliss: "That says it all."
**The BBC golf commentary team,
men of few words**

Golf

" This is the 12th, the green is like
a plateau with the top shaved off."
Renton Laidlaw goes a little flat

" Notices are appearing at courses telling
golfers not to lick their balls on the green."
**One commentator at the 1989 British Masters
golf tournament has got the double
entendre licked**

" I made the last putt. It just didn't go in."
**Golfer Tom Kite on the difference
between victory and defeat**

Ballesteros felt much better today after a 69.
**Is British golf commentator Renton Laidlaw
being naughty?**

Golf

" I owe a lot to my parents, especially
my mother and father."
**Golf legend Greg Norman seems
to have a lot of parents**

" If you'd offered me a 69 at the start
this morning I'd have been all over you."
**Golfer Sam Torrance seems
a little excitable**

Yes, Jean van de Velde is a clown,
another Frère Jacques Cousteau."
Oh, brother, is Tony Adamson mixed up!

> Birdies wherever you look. They're coming down like hailstones.
> **Former professional golfer Ken Brown**

" That's not a million miles away."
Peter Alliss

" Difficult couple of holes here – 15, 16 and 17."
Former golfer Howard Clark

" And on the eve of the Bob Hope Classic an interview with the man himself – Gerald Ford."
Mistaken identity by golf presenter Jim Rosenthal

" You couldn't find two more different personalities than these two men, Tom Watson and Brian Barnes. One the complete golf professional and the other the complete professional golfer."
Peter Alliss

Golf

" It's for all the gold in the world. "
Peter Alliss reckons there's a fortune in golf

" Was I intimated by Tiger Woods? A little bit.
He's got an aroma about him. "
Ben Curtis can sniff out a winner

" The par here at Sunningdale is 70
and anything under that will be a
score in the 60s. "
**Commentator Steve Rider
has his maths right**

He used to be fairly indecisive,
but now he's not so certain.
Peter Alliss

Golf

I can't see, unless the weather changes,
the conditions changing dramatically.
Peter Alliss

" What do I think of Tiger Woods? "
I don't know. I never played there.
Golfer Sandy Lyle

" He certainly didn't appear as cool as he looked. "
Renton Laidlaw

Azinger is wearing an all-black outfit:
black jumper, blue trousers, white shoes
and a pink tea-cosy hat.
Renton Laidlaw

Horse
Racing

Confusion in the heat of the moment as a race reaches its climax or uncertainty about whether they are referring to the horse or the rider, these are the obstacles faced by race commentators and pundits. Throw in such words as "hard", "soft" and "ride" and you can see why some have the occasional verbal fall.

Horse Racing

" She ran through the field like water
through a duck. "
**What sport was former jockey and
TV presenter John Francombe watching?**

" Well, you gave the horse a wonderful ride
– everybody saw that. "
Television presenter Des Lynam

" Princess Anne's horse is literally eating
up the ground. "
**A new diet for horse-racing correspondent
Peter Bromley**

" This is really a lovely horse.
I once rode her mother. "
Racing commentator Ted Walsh

" ...and there's the unmistakable figure
of Joe Mercer... or is it Lester Piggott? "
**Maybe horse-racing correspondent
Brough Scott needed glasses?**

" Tony has a quick look between his legs and likes what he sees. "
Winning Post's Stewart Machin speaks for all men

The racecourse is as level as a billiard ball.
A verbal balls-up here from Channel 4 horse-racing man John Francombe

" My word! Look at that magnificent erection. "
You would never have guessed that Brough Scott was talking about the new stand at Doncaster racecourse

" They usually have four or five dreams a night about coming from different positions. "
Former champion rider Willie Carson telling the BBC's Claire Balding how jockeys prepare for a big race

" A jockey without a whip is like a carpenter without a spanner. "

Frankie Dettori obviously wasn't a carpenter before he became a top jockey

He was going all right until he fell.
Jockey John Cullen

" This is the first time she has had 14 hands between her legs. "
John Francombe

" A lot of horses get distracted. It's just human nature. "
Horse trainer Nick Zito

" In this yard, all horses are treated equally, but there is one animal that knows he's a little more equal than the others. "
Equality comes unequally in a BBC News item about star horse Kauto Star event

" The bookies are literally waltzing
out of here under cloud nine. "
**Commentator Colm Murray at
the Cheltenham Festival**

" At Ascot today the heat is quite hot. "
**BBC presenter Judith Chalmers
at a flat-racing event**

It looks as though that premature excitement
may have been premature.
BBC racing man Brough Scott

" That's the magic of TV, I've just heard
over the headphones that Noalto was third. "
**Technology has been a mystery for the
BBC's David Coleman.**

Motorsport

In a few of the sports already featured one or two names keep cropping up, but nothing like to the degree that Murray Walker dominates motorsport commentary faux pas. His infectious enthusiasm, confused descriptions and gift for speaking without thinking make him a standout comic commentator. Add to this his apparent ability to jinx the driver he is discussing and you have a broadcaster whose "Murrayisms" will remain in sports commentary folklore forever.

Motorsport

" Do my eyes deceive me or is
Senna's Lotus sounding rough?"
**Aural cock-up from Grand Prix
commentator Murray Walker**

" Alboreto has dropped back up to fifth place."
**Murray Walker seems to have misplaced
a Formula One driver**

" I can't imagine what kind of problem Senna has.
I imagine it must be some sort of grip problem."
Murray Walker

" The drivers have one foot on the brake,
one on the clutch and one on the throttle."
**Speed Channel's Bob Varsha pedalling
some nonsense**

" It's basically the same, just darker."
**No change, then, for stock-car racer
Alan Kulwicki on switching Saturday
night racing to Sunday afternoons**

I kind of like to have someone looking up my arse.
**Former IndyCar and Formula One driver
Mario Andretti**

" Schumacher virtually pedalling
his Benetton back with his fists. "
**According to Murray Walker, the
German F1 driver was adding extra punch**

" There are enough Ferraris to eat
a plate of spaghetti. "
Former Grand Prix champion Jackie Stewart

" Ericsson's record is second to none in the
RAC Rally; he's been second three times. "
**A Mitsubishi Motors spokesman doesn't
quite get the point**

" He is shedding buckets of adrenalin in that car. "
Murray Walker makes it sound messy

Murray Walker: "So Bernie [Ecclestone], in the 17 years since you bought McLaren, which of your many achievements do you think was the most memorable?"

Bernie Ecclestone: "Well, I don't remember buying McLaren."

One team was obviously much the same as another for Walker, because Ecclestone owned Brabham

" A mediocre season for Nelson Piquet as he is now known and always has been. "
Murray Walker

Alain Prost is in a commanding second position.
Murray Walker

Motorsport

" Thackwell really can metaphorically
coast home now. "
Murray Walker

" What does it feel like being rammed
up the backside by Barrichello? "
**Commentator James Allen gets personal
when interviewing F1 driver Ralf Schumacher**

" And now Jacques Laffite is as close
to Surer as Surer is to Laffite. "
Murray Walker

" Nigel Mansell is the last person in the
race apart from the five in front of him. "
Murray Walker

" Speaking from memory, I don't know
how many points Nelson Piquet has. "
Murray Walker

Murray Walker: "What's that? There's a body on the track!!!"
Co-presenter: "Um, I think that that is a piece of bodywork, from someone's car."
Things are not always as they appear

Jenson (Button) is literally putting his balls on the line going up against Lewis.
Formula One summariser David Coulthard

" I don't want to tempt fate but Damon Hill is now only half a lap from his first Grand Prix win and… and… he's slowing down, Damon Hill is slowing down… he's… he's stopped. "
Did Murray Walker put the mockers on Hill?

" This is an interesting circuit because it has inclines, and not just up, but down as well. "
The ups and downs of being Murray Walker

Motorsport

" Cruel luck for Alesi, second on the grid. That's the first time he had started from the front row in a Grand Prix, having done so in Canada earlier this year. "
Murray Walker's knowledge is second to none

" And there's the man in the green flag! "
Murray Walker

" You can't see a digital clock because there isn't one. "
Murray Walker

Murray Walker: "And look at the flames coming from the back of Berger's McLaren."
Co-presenter: "Actually, Murray, they're not flames, it's the safety light."

... and there's no damage to the car... except to the car itself.
Murray Walker contradicts himself

Only a few more laps to go and then the action will begin, unless this is the action, which it is.
Murray Walker

" Tombay's hopes, which were nil before, are absolutely zero now. "
Murray Walker gets negative

" The Italian GP at Monaco... "
Geography's not Murray Walker's strong point sometimes

...the enthusiastic enthusiasts...
Grand Prix tautology from Murray Walker

" As you can see, visually, with your eyes... "
Can Grand Prix viewers see what Murray Walker is getting at?

Motorsport

" Andrea de Cesaris... the man who has won more Grands Prix than anyone else without actually winning one of them. "
A confused Murray Walker

And we have had five races so far this year, Brazil, Argentina, Imola, Schumacher and Monaco!
Murray Walker

" And Damon Hill is coming into the pit lane... yes, it's Damon Hill coming into the Williams pit, and Damon Hill in the pit... no, it's Michael Schumacher! "
A case of mistaken identity for Murray Walker

> Mansell is slowing it down, taking it easy.
> Oh no, he isn't! It's a lap record.
> **Murray Walker**

" Into lap 53, the penultimate last lap but one. "
Things don't add up for Murray Walker

" There are a lot of ifs in Formula One,
in fact IF is Formula One backwards! "
Murray Walker

" And that just shows you how important
the car is in Formula One racing. "
Murray Walker is dead right about that

" A battle is developing between them.
I say developing, because it's not yet on. "
Murray Walker gets his crystal ball out

" A sad ending, albeit a happy one. "
Murray Walker

Motorsport

" And Edson Arantes di Nascimento,
commonly known to us as Pelé,
hands the award to Damon Hill,
commonly known to us as Damon Hill."
Murray Walker

And Michael Schumacher is actually in
a very good position. He is in last place.
**Don't think Schumacher would agree
with Murray Walker**

" And now, excuse me while I interrupt myself."
Murray Walker

" Are they on a one-stopper? Are they on
a two? And when I say they, who do I mean?
Well, I don't know. It could be anybody."
**One of those confused days for
Murray Walker**

Ralf Schumacher speaking in German for our English listeners.
English listeners would have been as mystified as Eleanor Oldroyd obviously was

" Even in five years' time, he will still be four years younger than Damon Hill."
Murray Walker has got it figured...

" Fantastic! There are four different cars filling the first four places."
Murray Walker states the obvious

" He can't decide whether to leave his visor half open or half closed."
Murray Walker got it half right

I don't know what happened, but there was a major malmisorganisation problem there.
Murray Walker has a "malmisorganisation problem" with his mouth

" I should imagine that the conditions in
the cockpit are totally unimaginable. "
Murray Walker uses his imagination

" Either the car is stationary, or it's on the move. "
Murray Walker

I've no idea what Eddie Irvine's orders are,
but he's following them superlatively well.
Murray Walker

" If the gloves weren't off before,
and they were, they sure are now! "
Murray Walker

" Colin had a hard on in practice earlier,
and I bet he wished he had a hard on now. "
**No, really, World Superbike racing
commentator Jack Burnicle was talking
about Colin Edwards's tyre choice**

It looks as though this year there will be 17
Grands Prix for the World Championship,
compared with the traditional 17.
Murray Walker should check his notes

" Now he must not go the wrong way round
the circuit, and unless he can spin himself
stationary through 360 degrees I fail to
see how he can avoid doing so."
Murray Walker gets it wrong by degrees

" In 12th and 13th, the two Jaguars
of Eddie Irvine."
Murray Walker is seeing double

" Prost can see Mansell in his earphones."
**Murray Walker reckons Alain
had got eyes each side of his head**

Motorsport

" So this being Michael Schumacher's
10th race in his 151st year in F1. "
**Murray Walker makes Schumacher
a real veteran driver**

" The boot's on the other Schumacher now! "
Murray Walker

The lead car is unique, except for
the one behind it, which is identical.
Murray Walker

" There are seven winners of the Monaco
Grand Prix on the starting line today,
and four of them are Michael Schumacher. "
**Oh no! Murray Walker's seeing double
double now**

" There's so many celebrities on this grid,
I can hardly see the wood for the trees. "
Martin Brundle

" Veteran BBC commentator Murray Walker
said it was the blackest day for Grand Prix racing
since he had started covering the sport."
**This BBC Teletext news piece should have
been checked before transmission, it seems**

" Mark Blundell stops with his front
wheels stationary."
**Murray Walker can sense
a bit of inertia here**

Since I have been here at McLaren, we have never
really had an amazing rear end.
**Lewis Hamilton speaking about his car
– not the cheerleaders in the pit area**

" The first four cars are both on the same tyres."
**Murray Walker must have been a bit tyred
himself to broadcast this**

Red Bull will be really worried about the blue smoke coming from the back of Mark Webber.
Martin Brundle

" There's nothing wrong with
the car except that it's on fire. "
**Murray Walker fans the flames
of uncertainty**

" This will be Williams's first win
since the last time a Williams won. "
Murray Walker

" Well, now we have exactly the same
situation as at the beginning of the race,
only exactly the opposite. "
Murray Walker turns things upside down

Motorsport

" The gap between the two cars is 0.9 of a second,
which is less than one second. "
Murray Walker's got it figured

I wonder if Watson is in the
relaxed state of mind he's in.
Murray Walker

" Your luck goes up and down
like swings and roundabouts. "
**Former Grand Prix champion
James Hunt**

I make no apologies for their absence.
I'm sorry they're not here.
Murray Walker is sorry for himself

Motorsport

This is lap 54. After that, it's 55, 56, 57, 58 and 59.

You can count on Murray Walker's figures

" The faster he goes, the quicker he'll get to the pits. The slower he goes, the longer it will take. "

Murray Walker on the principles of speed

Tambay's hopes, which were nil before, are absolutely zero now.

Murray Walker

" You might not think that's cricket, and it's not, it's motor racing. "

Murray Walker thinks we might be confused about the difference

Motorsport

" The young Ralf Schumacher has been upstaged by the teenager Jensen Button, who is 20. "
Murray Walker got it a teen-y bit wrong

" He [Damon Hill] doesn't know – but if anyone knows he would. "
Don't know what Murray Walker knows about this

" Look up there! That's the sky! "
Murray Walker seems surprised

" You can cut the tension with a cricket stump. "
Murray Walker gets a bit heavy-handed

If that's not a lap record, I'll eat the hat I don't normally wear.
Murray Walker

That's history. I say history because it happened in the past.
Murray Walker gets nostalgic

" If McLaren hadn't gone for Jenson (Button), they'd have gone for someone else. "
There's no fooling Kimi Raikkonen's manager

Rugby

Cryptic commentary, daft insights, mixed-up metaphors and some unintentional innuendo form the bedrock of these rugby commentary calamities. Whether it is rugby league or union, these will have the scrum rolling in the mud with laughter.

Rugby

" If I've seen two more competitive players
than Armstrong and Van der Westheizen,
I've yet to see them. "
**An "are they or aren't they?" conundrum
for former Scotland rugby union captain
and pundit Gavin Hastings**

" This lad's a butcher – but I've never
had any of his meat. "
Rugby league commentator Eddie Waring

They've got their heads in the sand.
It's a Canute job.
**A mixed-up rugby union commentator
gets his metaphors in a twist**

" And the blue and white hoops of Sale will
no doubt act as a red flag to the Tigers. "
**Colourful commentary from the BBC's
Ian Brown**

And there's Gregor Townsend's knee,
looking very disappointed.
Gavin Hastings

" The ball is often a handicap in these conditions. "
**Former rugby player and commentator Nigel
Starmer-Smith finds his tongue a handicap, too**

" …and, in contrast, we have the New Zealand
team littered with internationals. "
**The BBC commentator has no surprises
for the Kiwis**

" I don't know where Jonny Wilkinson is.
I do know where he is, he's not there. "
Former rugby player Brian Moore

" Nigel Starmer-Smith had seven
craps for England some years ago. "
Presenter and pundit Jimmy Hill

Rugby

" Knowledge is knowing that a tomato is a fruit; wisdom is knowing not to put it in a fruit salad. "
Ireland's Brian O'Driscoll's hard-to-fathom answer when asked what it was like to play with fellow British and Irish Lion Martin Johnson

Reporter: "What of the future for Welsh rugby?"
Welsh captain Mike Watkins: "Over to the Angel for a lot of pints."

Condom is back in French pack.
Was this rugby union headline in *the Independent* newspaper in French letters?

" Rafter again doing much of the unseen work which the crowd relishes so much. "
Rugby commentator Bill McLaren

Rugby

" The French selectors never do anything by halves;
for the first international of the season against
Ireland they dropped half the three-quarter line. "
**Give Nigel Starmer-Smith half
a chance and he'll get it wrong**

" A lot of these guys have waited a
lifetime not to win this. "
**Aussie rugby union star David Campese had
waited a lifetime not to get this broadcast right**

" We go to the four corners of the globe
to bring you the best of rugby league
– Batley, Oldham, Wigan and France. "
**Geography lesson needed for
commentator Eddie Hemmings**

" We all know England are the best rugby team in the
world and next weekend, when they play Scotland,
we'll find out if they are the best in Britain. "
Lord Archer obviously rates Britain highly

Rugby

" Scotland were victims of their own failure."
Gavin Hastings

" We are committing our own suicide."
Suicide is so personal for Scotland rugby union team coach Ian McGeechan

" Hopefully the rain will hold off for both sides."
Unbiased rain – just what rugby union star Lawrence Dallaglio wanted

They're a bit laxative.
Rugby league's Robbie Paul is a bit lackadaisical with words

" Andrew Mehrtens loves it when Daryl Gibson comes inside of him."
New Zealand rugby commentator's vocal slip-up

Rugby

… and Dusty Hare kicked 19 of the 17 points.
David Coleman covers rugby for a change and struggles with the scoring system

" Frustration was the buzzword in the squad on Saturday."
Former England coach Martin Johnson

" We have self-belief in each other."
A very believable Gavin Hastings

" The ref's turned a blind ear."
New Zealand rugby union commentator Murray Mexted

" And he's got the icepack on his groin there, so possibly not the old shoulder injury."
That medical degree came in handy for commentator Ray French

Rugby

" I don't like this new law, because your first instinct when you see a man on the ground is to go down on him. "
Murray Mexted

" I am not getting any younger and there are a few other guys in the same situation. "
Age begins to tell on England's Nick Easter

" You don't like to see hookers going down on players like that. "
Double-entendre specialist Murray Mexted strikes again...

He's looking for some meaningful penetration into the backline.
... and again...

Rugby

" Everybody knows that I have
been pumping Martin Leslie for
a couple of seasons now."
Another Murray Mexted classic

There's no such thing as a lack of confidence.
You either have it or you don't.
England rugby international Rob Andrew

" I just love it when Mehrtens
comes on the inside of Marshall."
Murray Mexted can't stop himself

Snooker

Perhaps these are a commentators' cries for help or just for their own amusement as they are forced to report on an intense game from a dark, clammy studio for hours on end. Whatever the reason, though, snooker has blessed this book with daft sporting quotes in abundance.

> 99 times out of 1,000 he would have potted that ball.
>
> **Snooker commentator Ted Lowe**

" And [Terry] Griffiths has looked at that blue four times now – and it still hasn't moved. "

Ted Lowe expects Griffiths to do great things with his eyes but wouldn't a cue be easier?

" He's lucky in one sense and lucky in the other. "

Ted Lowe

" What Graeme Dott likes to do is win frames. "

Snooker's Steve Davis

" The audience are literally electrified and glued to their seats. "

Sticky situation for Ted Lowe

Snooker

" Oh, that's a brilliant shot. The odd thing
is his mum's not very keen on snooker. "
Ted Lowe

" [Alex] Higgins first entered the championship
10 years ago. That was for the first time,
of course. "
Ted Lowe chalks up a definite first

" And it is my guess that Steve Davis will try to
score as many points as he can in this frame. "
**Ted Lowe has at least got the point of
snooker nailed down**

" Steve Davis has a tough consignment in
front of him. "
Ted Lowe

A little pale in the face, but then his name
is White.
Ted Lowe a little red-faced over this comment?

Snooker

" That pot puts the game beyond reproach. "
Ted Lowe goes in for the blame game

" All square, all the way round. "
Ted Lowe squares the circle

" There is, I believe, a time limit for playing a shot.
But I think it's true to say that nobody knows
what the limit is. "
Ted Lowe needs a rule book

" Jimmy White has that wonderful gift of being
able to point his cue where he is looking. "
**Ted Lowe reckons there's no room for cross-
eyed snooker players, then?**

When you start off, it's usually nil-nil.
Former snooker champion Steve Davis

Snooker

" Just enough points here for Tony
to pull the cat out of the fire. "
**Can TV snooker commentator Ray Edmonds
smell burning fur somewhere?**

" Suddenly Alex Higgins is 7–0 down. "
**TV snooker commentator David Vine
seemed to have lost track of time**

" Tony Meo is beginning to find his potting boots. "
**Former player and snooker commentator
Rex Williams**

" From this position you've got to fancy
either yourself or your opponent winning. "
**Snooker player and pundit Kirk Stevens
sits on the fence**

" The match has gradually and suddenly
come to a climax. "
David Vine isn't too sure about this, though

Snooker

" No one came closer to winning the
title last year than the runner-up. "
**Former snooker player and commentator
Dennis Taylor**

" I've always said the difference between
winning and losing in nothing at all. "
Snooker legend Terry Griffiths

" Valour was the better part of discretion there. "
**TV snooker commentator Jack Karnehm
mixes his metaphors**

" Sometimes the deciding frame is
always the hardest one to win. "
Dennis Taylor

" That said, the inevitable failed to happen. "
**TV snooker commentator John Pulman
was inevitably wrong about that**

Snooker

10–4 and that could mean exactly what it means.
Well, David Vine knows what HE means

" And now for some snooker news: Steve Davis has
crashed out of the UK Billiards Championship. "
**Snooker player and commentator Allan Taylor
gets his green baize sports mixed up**

" Ray Reardon is one of the great Crucible
champions. He won it five times when
the championship was played away
from the Crucible. "
David Vine misses his own point

" And that's the third time this session he's
missed his waistcoat pocket with the chalk. "
Eagle-eyed Ted Lowe

" There are those with commentators'
eyes, and then there's Willie Thorne. "
John Virgo

> Steve is going for the pink ball – and for those of you who are watching in black and white, the pink is next to the green.
>
> **Colourful commentary from Ted Lowe**

" Jimmy White is known as 'The Nearly Man' of snooker, but a lot of people forget that he's got the second best record in the world championship in the 1990s."
Does snooker ace Steve Davis reckon White is second to none?

" At certain times here, and even in the hotel, there's nearly a stench of death in the place."
Snooker is life and death for Irish star Fergal O'Brien

" For those of you watching who do not have TV sets, live commentary is on Radio 2."
Ted Lowe mystifies viewers and listeners

Snooker

" Fred Davis, the doyen of snooker. Now 67 years
of age and too old to get his leg over, prefers
to use his left hand. "
**Commentator Ted Lowe was referring
to snooker, of course**

If you get to 9-7... you start seeing alarm bells then.
Commentator John Parrot

" It's all about the length and this one doesn't
look hard enough to me. "
Is John Virgo being rude?

" This is where the precision has to be precise. "
**Former snooker player John Spencer
knows precisely**

" That's inches away from being millimetre perfect. "
**Looks like snooker commentator Ted Lowe
is got stuck somewhere between imperial
and metric**

Tennis

In this chapter you will find some marvellous examples of commentators and players stating the blindingly obvious. Whether they feel they are doing the general public a service or perhaps just desperately trying to fill some airtime in a long and uneventful match, I am not sure. All I know is that the volley of queer quotes makes for hilarious reading.

Tennis

And here's Zivojinovic, six feet six inches tall and 14 pounds 10 ounces.
BBC tennis commentator Dan Maskell makes light of the player

" Martina, she's got several layers of steel out there, like a cat with nine lives. "
Wimbledon champion and BBC tennis commentator Virginia Wade's analogies can be a bit bewildering

The Gullikson twins here. An interesting pair, both from Wisconsin.
Dan Maskell

" It's quite clear that Virginia Wade is thriving on the pressure now that the pressure on her to do well is off. "
BBC commentator Harry Carpenter's on-off comments

Tennis

" Billie Jean King, with the look on her face
that says she can't believe it... because she never
believes it, and yet, somehow, I think she does. "
**Unbelievable comments from BBC
tennis pundit Max Robertson**

" I'm an American. You can't go on where
you were born. If you do, then John McEnroe
would be a German. "
**Pundit and tennis legend Martina Navratilova
misplaces Mac's heritage**

" As Boris Becker sits there, his eyes staring out in
front of him, I wonder what he's thinking. I think
he's thinking, 'I am Boris Becker.' At least I hope
that's what he's thinking. "
**Methinks the BBC's John Barrett wasn't
thinking before he started speaking...**

" Miss Stove seems to be going off the boil. "
Tennis commentator Peter West likes a pun

" You can always feel much better if someone endorses the call – even if they are wrong. "
Virginia Wade

Sampras's heart must have been in his hands.
I've heard of wearing your heart on your leeve but this Sky commentator sees more

" I wonder if the Germans have a word for *Blitzkrieg* in their language. "
Achtung! **A language gaffe from South African tennis pundit Frew McMillan**

" Nobody is blaming the linesman. Of course, he did make a couple of big mistakes. Really big ones. "
Tennis star Marat Saffin makes his point on officialdom

Tennis

" I have a feeling that, if she had been playing herself, she would have won that point. "
Former Australian tennis player and commentator Bob Hewitt

" Getting your first serve in is a great way to avoid double faults. "
Former Australian tennis player John Fitzgerald serves up the obvious for tennis fans

Martina Hingis is going through a part of her life which she has never been through before.
BBC tennis commentator

" Federer is human, but for how long? "
BBC tennis commentator

If you can't get near a radio, Henman's taken the first set.

A bit of radio ga-ga from BBC Radio

" Sampras, in white, serves with his baggy shorts. "

The BBC's Ian Carter has a theory about why Pete's balls were nearly always in

" These ball boys are marvellous. You don't even notice them. There's a left-handed one over there. I noticed him earlier. "

Max Robertson

" She never loses a match. If she loses a match, it's because her opponent beats her. "

Former tennis player and commentator Pam Shriver seemed a little confused

Tennis

" She comes from a tennis-playing family.
Her father's a dentist. "
BBC commentator

" Well, judging from his serves, Larsson
will either win this match or lose it. "
**A Eurosport commentator was definitely
hedging his bets**

Tennis is one of those games like all other games.
**Wimbledon champion Virginia Wade doesn't
think tennis is unique**

Other
Sports

Unintentional sports slip-ups happen in all sports. American football, baseball, basketball, darts, Gaelic football and weightlifting have all made hilarious contributions to the compendium of comic commentary.

In cycling you can put all your money
on one horse.
**Cycling legend Stephen Roche
changes saddles.**

" And this is Gregoriava from Bulgaria. I saw
her snatch this morning and it was amazing!"
Weightlifting commentator Pat Glenn

" Teddy McCarthy to John McCarthy,
no relation, John McCarthy back to
Teddy McCarthy, still no relation..."
**Gaelic football commentator Michael
O'Muircheartaigh**

" He's been burning the midnight oil at both ends."
Darts expert Sid Waddell by the sound of it

" This seesaw's going up and down like a roundabout,
what a match!"
Sid Waddell

Other Sports

" What a man, what a lift, what a jerk! "
**Jimmy McGee on weightlifting in
the Olympic Games**

" ...and so they have not been able
to improve their 100 per cent record. "
BBC Sports Round-up

" Only one word for it – magic darts. "
Darts commentator Tony Green

" 3–0 Finland and Russia are lucky to get nothing. "
**No credit for the Russians from the
BBC's ice hockey commentator**

" If our swimmers want to win any more medals,
they'll have to put their skates on. "
Does Dave Brenner want swimming on ice?

" I can't tell who's leading. It's either Oxford
or Cambridge. "
**John Snagge seems to have eyesight problems
during the Oxford and Cambridge boat race**

Rapport? You mean like, 'You run as fast as you can, and I'll throw it as far as I can?'
Jeff Kemp, 49ers football quarterback, simplifies his relationship with wide receiver Jerry Rice

" I'm not allowed to comment on lousy officiating. "
Jim Finks, New Orleans Saints general manager, pushes his luck with officialdom

" When you get that nice celebration coming into the dugout and you're getting your ass hammered by guys – there's no better feeling than to have that done. "
Is baseball star Matt Stairs revealing too many secrets

" The doctors X-rayed my head and found nothing. "
Baseball legend Dizzy Dean

Other Sports

" I was glad to see Italy win. All the guys
on the team were Italians. "
**Why does Tom Lasorda, former Dodgers
manager, find that surprising for Italy's
World Cup team?**

This is like deja vu all over again.
**Former New York Yankees player Yogi
Berra had a safer pair of hands than
his mouth has been.**

" Predictions are difficult. Especially
about the future. "
Yogi Berra gets tongue-tied again

" He must have made that before he died. "
Yogi Berra referring to a Steve McQueen movie

" I take a two-hour nap, from one o'clock to four. "
Time just flies for Yogi Berra

Other Sports

" Ralph, I would like to be able to tell the folks what happened on that play, but the Florida cheerleaders were shaking their fuzzy things right in front of us. "
University of Kentucky commentator Cawood Ledford clearly gets distracted by pom poms

" He dribbles a lot and the opposition doesn't like it. In fact you can see it all over their faces. "
A performance that had an NBC analyst salivating

" I've never had major knee surgery on any other part of my body. "
NBA star Winston Bennett

" I'm not a big Gay guy. "
Pundit Rick Majerus was stating his player, rather than sexual, preference about college player Rudy Gay.

" When you come to a fork in the road, take it! "
Baseball's Yogi Berra speaks with forked tongue

> Rich Folkers is throwing up in the bullpen.
> **Former baseball player and commentator**
> **Jerry Coleman thinks he might be sick**
> **of baseball**

" Always go to other people's funerals;
otherwise they won't go to yours. "
Yogi Berra

" Baseball is 90 per cent mental. The other half is physical. "
Yogi Berra has a maths problem

" I told him, 'Son, what is it with you.
Is it ignorance or apathy?' He said,
'Coach, I don't know and I don't care.' "
Utah Jazz president Frank Layden's
exchange with a player

" Left hand, right hand, it doesn't matter.
I'm amphibious. "
Former pro Charles Shackleford
might be a handy guy to swim with

He has the players too happy.
**Boston Celtics' general manager Red
Auerbach is critical of Bill Russell's coaching**

Reporter: "Did you visit the Parthenon
while in Greece?"
Basketball star Shaquille O'Neill:
"I can't really remember the names
of all the clubs we went to."

" My sister's expecting a baby, and I don't know
if I'm going to be an uncle or an aunt."
**Relationships aren't a strong point for
North Carolina State player Chuck Nevitt**

He treats us like men. He lets us wear earrings.
**Houston University receiver Torrin Polk
is so grateful to his coach**